A Story of a True Hero

by

Jose C. Soriano

DORRANCE PUBLISHING CO., INC.
PITTSBURGH, PENNSYLVANIA 15222

The contents of this work including, but not limited to, the accuracy of events, people, and places depicted; opinions expressed; permission to use previously published materials included; and any advice given or actions advocated are solely the responsibility of the author, who assumes all liability for said work and indemnifies the publisher against any claims stemming from publication of the work.

ISBN: 978-1-4349-0313-6
Printed in the United States of America

First Printing

For more information or to order additional books,
please contact:
Dorrance Publishing Co., Inc.
701 Smithfield Street
Pittsburgh, Pennsylvania 15222
U.S.A.
1-800-788-7654
www.dorrancebookstore.com

Dedication

To my wife, Flor, and our son Joseph and his wife Fe and newborn baby Draven Kaleo, and Jonathan.
Thank you for the encouragement and support.
You're the best in the world and I love you.

To my wife, Flor, and our sons, Joseph and Jonathan.
Thank you for the encouragement and support.
You're the best in the world and I love you.

While watching *CNN Headline News* one evening, I saw a soldier from World War II being recognized and finally receiving the Congressional Medal of Honor he deserved. This prompted me to write a true story of heroism about my grandmother, Aguida Lolarga Castro, and her family during World War II. When I was young, my grandfather, with tears in his eyes, told us an incredible story about my grandmother. Even though I did not see my grandmother, I believe she was a true hero.

When I was born, my father was serving the mighty U.S. Navy in the Pacific, and Mother suffered emotional distress or post-traumatic syndrome because of her husband's frequent time spent away from home. She couldn't take care of me, so she ditched me, giving me to my grandfather for care. My grandfather's name is Emeterio Castro. He was a tall athletic person of Spanish descent and dedicated to his family. He often behaved liked a nincompoop to humor his family and friends.

My grandfather devoted his faith to our Almighty God, and every Sunday we went to church and sat in the front pew to be the first in line for communion. My grandparents had eight children, and after the war, my grandfather struggled to raise them on his own. My mother's name is Angelina, and she is the third child in the family. The children's names are Marcial, Amanda, Angelina, Tony, Antonio, Carling, Gerardo, and Ernesto.

At daybreak my grandfather woke me up and we traveled to his secluded dwelling where he tended his duck farm, a barn where hundreds of ducks were corralled for the night leaving their eggs littered on the ground. You had to be careful roaming around the barn or otherwise you were subjected to eat the eggs you broke. He selected the equally sized eggs and placed them with the nesting duck for incubation. A few days later he harvested and boiled and "Balut" was born. Filipinos are crazy for "Balut" eggs. They're a delicacy so they say, and a male aphrodisiac.

Aside from his duck farm, he tended his poultry and livestock. He had enormous property, and near his secluded dwelling was a lake where his animals spent their time wallowing. Next to the barn was a huge tree where he constructed his club house, located above. The view from his clubhouse was spectacular. Adjacent to his barn was a log beam where he practiced his rock-throwing skills. Buckets and buckets of sizeable rocks were on the side of his barn, along with empty cans and bottles which he used to practice his skills. I was impressed when I saw my grandfather hit a bird in the air.

My grandfather has been a rock thrower since he was a kid, and he was taught by his father. During the Spanish occupation of the Philippines, my grandfather was unbeatable. He was fast and accurate executing his target. The Spaniards were impressed by my grandfather's capability, and his popularity traveled the globe.

In challenge after challenge he faced various local and Spanish champions and competitors in the country, and he earned the respect of his adversaries. My grandfather's left hand was longer than his right hand, and I guess it's the result of the long time he spent rock throwing.

One Sunday afternoon, I was playing near the lake when a humongous dragon reptile chased the ducks laying eggs on the ground. I was scared and yelled out to my resting grandfather swaying in the hammock. Without hesitation, he asked me to stay still and fired several shots at the feasting dragon, and it was a bullseye. The reptile's carcass splattered into pieces and blood spewed onto my shirt. I picked up the tail and tossed it in the lake.

He patiently taught me how to throw rocks, but I wasn't gifted at it, and the next day I suffered excruciating pain in my shoulder and never tried to do it again.

It was my grandfather's birthday, and I gave him a bottle of gin as a present. After drinking the entire bottle of gin, my grandfather gave me a big hug and he said, "Thank you, grandson. Now I am drunk." He said, "I know the reason why you gave that bottle of gin: Aha, you want me to spill the story of your grandmother." This is the story of my grandparents.

In the year 1945, one evening my grandparents were having supper when a big bang erupted nearby. The loud impact panicked everyone, and they zinged out to the hiding location.

Frazzled by the incident, they waited for a moment to see if Japanese soldiers were present in the area. Gently they crawled and peeked through the crevices to see what was happening outside. The visibility was poor, but flames were visible in the distance. A heavy downpour helped extinguish the fire. Smoke still bellowed aloft, and my grandparents were curious to find out what was going on. They carefully approached the crash site, and they heard a cry of someone uttering for help, but my grandparents were afraid to get too close because it was probably another Japanese trick. A man's voice desperately called for helped. They moved closer, and my grandmother recognized the star insignia of the plane, and instantaneously she was hollering and calling her children to help the wounded Americans. In their Pangasinan dialect she said, "*Amerikano, Amerikano, apera yo, apera yo tulongan yo ra tay Americano ta pia no' nai-salva-tira tampol.*"

It's translated, "Hurry, hurry, help the wounded Americans." The family acted like super humans, and immediately the three Americans were safe and out of the wreckage, except for the one officer in the rear of the plane who was completely charred beyond recognition. His name was Officer Putnam. Officer Putnam specialized in mapping and sketching enemy locations and aerial photography. The surviving Americans suffered severe injuries. The pilot and the co-pilot were pinned underneath the dashboard, suffering broken legs; and the other officer, sitting behind the cockpit was impaled with a metal object mere inches from his heart. My grandfather said Officer Waget was "African-American," Officer Chelos was an "American Indian," and Officer Anderson was Caucasian. They were USAF photo surveillance, mapping the Japanese locations in Pangasinan Province for an American invasion in Lingayen Beach. The USAF photo surveillance crew was on their way back to the base somewhere on Corregidor Island when lightning hit the tail of the plane, and it went out of control, and crashed.

Officer Putnam always said, "If I die, I'd rather die up here aloft rather than dying out there with a bunch of Japanese butchering your throat with their bayonets." It was an indescribable scene, my grandfather said, but it's a miracle the three Americans survived the crash.

My grandmother used coconut juice and herbal concoctions to dress their wounds, to stop the bleeding, and to protect them against infections. My grandmother had no training in the medical field, but she did an excellent job caring for the wounded Americans. Everyone in the family contributed their efforts to save the Americans. The children improvised bamboo sticks to use for tourniquets.

My grandfather was already panicking and afraid the Japanese soldiers were on their way, but my grandmother was relaxed, tending to the wounded American soldiers.

"Everything is rush, rush, rush," my grandmother said. "Do not worry, my husband, the Japanese are stocked somewhere down the road, everything is flooded, so it will take them days to get over here," she added as she hummed *The Star Spangled Banner.*

Again my grandfather was all stressed and worried. He called his children to prepare the sleigh for the water buffalo or Carabao to get ready to transport the Americans to the hideout location.

My grandparents' dwelling was made of Nipa hut or palm leaf materials. The children knew exactly what needed to be done for everyone's safety, and everything was ready to be mobilized. One of the children was up above the treetops observing enemy activities in the vicinities.

Probably at this time the Japanese troops were already on their way. Villagers appeared in the distance, but were afraid to get nearby because of the heavy downpour and the constant strikes of lightning and thunder rattling the heavens. The child above in the tree alerted everyone on the ground someone was coming.

It was the Barrio Kapitan who emerged from the bushes, rushed into the house and rendered help to the wounded Americans. The Barrio Kapitan's name was Danilo Macaraeg and everyone knew him in the village as "Kapitan Danilo." Kapitan Danilo was an informant monitoring the Japanese activities in the area and transmitted all information to the Philippine guerilla in the region. Immediately Kapitan Danilo transmitted the message in the air by drumming bamboo planks.

The Japanese were scrambling to decode the signal, but unfortunately they were illiterate in understanding the code. In town the Japanese soldiers broadcast their intentions, offering money, food, and freedom for anyone who could help them decode the message. When no one came forward to help the Japanese decode the signals, the killings began. Too many deaths in one day littered the street with innocent people's bodies.

Behind the town's municipal building were hundreds of corpses buried in a shallow grave. It's a horrifying site to describe, my grandfather said, because many of his friends were among the dead buried in that shallow grave. During the monsoon season, the rain exhumed the remains out of the shallow grave, and they were swept by the strong current and littered the riverbanks.

My grandparents didn't think of themselves or their well-being. Their main concern was to save the Americans in harm's way.

Somewhere down the road, the Japanese were already embarking.

Kapitan Danilo helped my grandparents to evacuate the wounded Americans to the safe location, and he vouched he would do anything to help the wounded Americans. Kapitan Danilo was a bit concerned as to where to hide the Americans. My grandparents informed Kapitan Danilo not to worry as everything was taken care of. He was to just follow along and he would see where the Americans would be housed to recuperate from their injuries.

The hideout location was a secret place, and only my grandparents knew the area. It was about six kilometers from their house, and it was a sacred place. During the Spanish occupation in the Philippines, the Spaniards hired thousands of Filipino workers to chisel the large boulder to create a subterranean passage down below. When the construction was finished the Spaniards killed every one of the Filipino workers and buried them deep beneath the ground, along with their gold and treasures of Filipino artifact. Many tried their luck to find the treasures, but they have vanished. My grandparents found a way to make the cave useful by storing their harvest, like rice or corn and other things, during the rainy season. The cave was spacious, and it had running water filtered through the limestone. But before entering the cave, you had to make an offering. My grandfather said the cave had something on it, like it was alive and protected the people who believed in it. After the Japanese found out the location and found evidence of the Americans' presence in the area, the Japanese blew the cave to smithereens.

Kapitan Danilo remained in the cave assisting the wounded Americans, and my grandparents had to go back to their house before Japanese soldiers arrived. On the way home, my grandparents made a promise to each other that no matter what happened, they had to do whatever it took to save the wounded Americans.

It was 10 P.M. when my grandparents arrived in the house from the cave. My grandmother asked her husband to get the children out of the house right away and bring them to their relatives in the next barrio. The children understood the situation, and they knew what to do.

My grandparents prepared for the children's needs for the dangerous journey. Palm leaves were plentiful to shade the children from the rain. It was already 11 P.M.

when my grandfather left the house with his children. Time was of the essence. A heavy downpour made their journey difficult, but my grandfather continued his trip for the safety of the children. The family arrived safely at the relative's next *barrio*, and my grandfather vowed to his children he would come back soon.

While my grandmother was waiting for her husband to come home, she went back to the crash site to salvage useful items for the Americans. With a lamp in her hand and palm leaves for shade, she walked towards the crash site.

The visibility was poor, but she was persistent to collect whatever she could salvage to help the Americans. She persevered.

As she approached the crash site, her peripheral view spotted an apparition of a man standing next to the fuselage. She stepped back down and killed the fire right away. She thought a Japanese presence was already in progress. She moved backward slowly away from the crash site when lightning lit the wreckage and showed nobody there. Goose bumps engulfed her body as she had to decide if she would continue to go on or turn around and head home.

To satisfy her curiosity, she entered the crippled plane, and the smell of cigarette smoke entered her nostrils. She reached in her pocket to light up the lamp, but the matchstick was moist, and now she depended on the frequent lightning flashes to see her way. She continued rummaging through the dilapidated plane and felt as if someone were watching her every move. She murmured to herself.

Feeling uncomfortable inside, she immediately got up and made her way out of the plane, but she tripped in the aisle and stumbled next to the corpse. She was petrified and screamed her lungs out. She extended her arms, reaching the handle bar to pull herself up, and again her hand slipped off the handle bar and the corpse fell off her, breaking into pieces. The skull bounced and wobbled on the seat. She was shaken, and extremely frightened as she wiped debris off of her face. She got up and proceeded out the door, but she hit her forehead against the overhead fixture, lost her balance, and fell onto the un-upholstered seat as the skull chaotically bounced in the air and landed in her lap.

She tossed the skull out of the plane, and quickly made her way out the door, panting. She continued murmuring, cursing, and otherwise expressing her emotions. Frequent lightning strikes reflected the shine of a metal object behind the cockpit. Right away she picked up the object, cleared the debris off, and carried it outside the skeleton plane. She was excited to open the metal object to see its contents. She pulled matches out of her pocket to light the lamp she was carrying, but the matchsticks were still moist. She attempted several times to light up the lamp, but unfortunately it was drizzling and the wind was picking up. As she proceeded to carry the metal object home, she stepped on an object. She picked it up, and it was a Zippo lighter. "It's a miracle," she said.

Frequent lightning strike made it easier for her to see her path and spot a Japanese presence in the area. She carried the box home and made sure no one was following her. She lit the lamp and viewed the name inscribed on the lighter: Lt. Bobby Putnam. She felt goose bumps all over her. She gently opened the metal box, and the contents were intact. There were two loaded forty-five caliber pistols, a knife, chocolate bars, a letter, pictures, cigarettes, and a sketch map of the enemy location in Lingayen Beach. Her heart palpitated rapidly, and she was overjoyed with what she discovered.

The night deepened and the weather was horrible, but nothing stopped her from getting to the cave to bring the good news to the wounded Americans.

The Americans were surprised by her sudden presence in the cave. 'Kapitan Danilo had already left and he would be back the next morning. My grandmother handed the Americans the box she'd found at the crash site. The Americans thought they'd lost the box forever and were afraid the box would end up in the enemy's hand.

The metal box had precious cargo: Officer Putnam had sketched a drawing detailing the enemy locations in Pangasinan Province and Lingayen Beach, where American troops would land to eradicate the Japanese presence in the area.

After a short conversation with the wounded Americans, my grandmother urgently left the cave to be with her husband.

On my grandfather's arrival back from the barrio at about, 1 A.M., he encountered some Japanese troops patrolling the area. He was frightened that he might be seen, so he quickly hid nearby in bushes and climbed to the top of the coconut tree. The rain stopped and he stayed there, patiently waiting for the soldiers to pass by, but instead the Japanese rested at the trunk of the coconut tree, chatting and smoking cigarettes. Up above in the tree, my grandfather was motionless.

An hour passed by, and the soldiers seemed to be having a good time chatting. Then all of a sudden, it turned solemn. Flashing lightning cleared his view down below. The Japanese soldiers rested comfortably. The skies continued flashing lightning bolts and winds blew steadily. He gently made his move down the tree. Half way down the trunk, one Japanese soldier got up and urinated nearby as my grandfather nervously held his grip steady. He feared that the Japanese might see him. He prayed for a miracle to save him. The soldier went back to sleep. Grandfather hurled his way up and waited for the right moment. He could hear the loud snores of the soldiers below as my grandfather gently worked his way down and bypassed the sleeping beauties. It was already dawn when he got home. He hugged his wife for the longest time, both in tears, asking themselves if they were doing the right thing.

Awakened by rumbling footsteps, my grandparents knew what was coming and remained calm. Multiple gunshots fired in the air to warn people not to escape. Japanese soldiers barricaded the crash site and rounded up everyone in the barrio. The Japanese soldiers furiously searched house to house and burned them. Others remained in their houses in hiding and burned to death. Some tried to escape, but they were gunned down. The Japanese soldiers ordered everyone to sit on the ground with their hands behind their heads, and they were told to speak only if asked.

An officer named Tanaka was furious and determined to find the remaining surviving Americans and punish them by decapitating their heads. Officer Tanaka warned that everyone helping or harboring the Americans would be harshly punished by decapitation. When none of the Filipinos came forward to testify about the incident, Officer Tanaka viciously smashed the American skull on the ground by stomping on it with his boots. He grabbed an innocent man and beheaded him to demonstrate to the people that he meant business. "Hand over the Americans now," Officer Tanaka said, "and you will be rewarded. We will spare everyone's lives."

Officer Tanaka asked who was the Barrio Kapitan in the village. Kapitan Danilo raised his hand. Officer Tanaka said, "are you aware, Kapitan, you are helping the enemy? We are your friends, we are your new government, so you will obey us and honor your Majesty Emperor Hirohito."

Kapitan Danilo responded harshly cursing the Japanese. Officer Tanaka responded viciously with a hard blow to Kapitan Danilo's chest, resulting in difficulty breathing as he held his chest in excruciating pain. Then another Japanese hit him with his rifle, knocking him on to the ground, unconscious. A bucket of water partially awakened him, though he was sluggish. Officer Tanaka shoved Kapitan Danilo on the ground and squashed his face with his boots as Kapitan Danilo's nose merely emerged to breath. Again and again officer Tanaka questioned Kapitan Danilo regarding the whereabouts of the Americans. He was lifted off the ground and given a chance to talk.

Kapitan Danilo spoke out loud to the Filipinos in his language: *"Huwag kay - ong magsalita o maki-koopirasyon sa mga hayop na Japon. Tayo'y magka-isa at ipaglaban natin ang ating bayan hanggang kamatayan."* It meant, "Do not talk or cooperate with the animal Japanese. We fight for our country until death. Do not say anything, we are one Filipinos."

The ruthless, draconian, atrocious Japanese Officer un-scabbarded his Samurai and beheaded the Barrio Kapitan instantly. His head rolled to the ditch, and a soldier picked it up and paraded it for everyone to see. Everyone was frightened and feared for their lives. People couldn't stomach the scene, and others tried to run away, but they were shot to death. Bodies of innocent children, the elderly, young couples, uncles and aunts, were littered everywhere. My grandparents, terribly in shock, trembled to see many dead people in a glimpse.

In the early years before the Japanese occupation of the Philippines, my grandfather remembered the Japanese Officer Tanaka. He often saw him at Calaciao or San Carlos, Pangasinan, on every Saturday doing business with the locals, buying and selling.

He blended in and communicated speaking broken Tagalog. No one expected him to be a monstrous killer. Japanese foreigners infested the country, pretending to be business entrepreneurs, but they were there to spy and invade the country. Filipinos didn't have a clue that the Japanese were already in position to seize the country until it was too late.

The Japanese corralled hundreds of families. Japanese soldiers selected young wenches 16–25 years old and transported them into a dinghy boat to an undisclosed location. Many young girls clung to their parents, but were forced and taken away. A young man ran after his girlfriend and they impaled him by bayonet. The Japanese soldiers placed bamboo planks behind everyone's backs and tightly tied their hands together and roped everyone at their necks like animals to prevent prisoners from escaping—even the children. Rain continued to pour as the soldiers dragged the people to town. Anyone refusing to walk was shot. As the march continued, people lost their balanced due to exhaustion, hunger, and weakness. The first day alone while marching to town, of two hundred of them, thirty-six people vanished while crossing the rapid creek. The children especially fell victim as ten of them were swallowed by the strong current. After a grueling ten hours of treacherous marching, they reached the town and were thrown into a pigpen. They were treated like animals and fed gooey rice soup.

The next day, the water was chest deep, and bodies of children and innocent people were swept away by the current. My grandparents clung to one another as they watched the water recede for two days. Many Filipinos did not survive the intense weather or hypothermia. The survivors were transferred to a holding facility and interrogated, and the weak ones were dumped in a pit and left to die.

One by one they were interrogated in different rooms, and the chilling sounds coming from the rooms was terrifying. The punishment was so severe that many of them didn't make it. A high-ranking Japanese officer offered anyone's freedom to leave if they would cooperate and work with the Japanese Imperial Army in capturing the Americans, but no one came forward.

After one week of brutal interrogation, they were only forty-eight people left, including my grandparents. My grandfather was punished severely with an open wound to his head and cuts and bruises everywhere, and my grandmother was raped. Children received lashes on their bodies.

A few days passed without rain, and water was scarce. Sweltering heat, thirst, and hunger contributed to everyone's psychological nightmares, especially the children and the elderly. The ground was saturated and knee-deep in mud. Bacteria, diseases, and creepy night crawlers were a menace to everyone. Everyone cried for food and water, especially the children, but the Japanese soldiers seemed to enjoy the outcome and burst with laughter, frolicking.

A mother breastfeeding her child was forced by the soldiers into a secluded room and raped. The sound of a women being raped by the soldiers was horribly terrifying, my grandfather said.

The simultaneous cries of the children inside the holding facility drove the Japanese soldiers crazy. Several Japanese soldiers fired in the air to stop the children from crying. As days went by, people slowly died from malnutrition. Others collected their own urine to ease their thirst and for their babies. During the night, hundreds of rats preyed on open wounds, and my grandfather found a way to trap the rats to sustain their hunger. Abundant night crawlers infested the holding cell, and the children found a way to have easy snacks.

At the holding area, a child continued to cry and a Japanese soldier asked the women to stop her baby from crying. She begged the soldier for a cup of his soup for her baby, but the soldier paid no attention to her. Again and again the women begged for rice soup for her baby, but there was no response. Then another soldier came inside the room with a bowl of soup. The soldier said, "Come and get it." She got up with her baby in her hand to get the bowl of soup when the soldier threw the soup onto her face. The rice soup splattered on her body and dripped on the floor as the lady crawled down, using her mouth to suck the mushy beads of rice soup and smooching it to her baby's mouth.

The soldier laughed, finding it funny to watch a woman gracing the ground. The soldier continued laughing out loud when the women got up and spewed her mouth on the soldier's face. The soldier swung his hand, knocking her to the ground. She responded angrily, saying in Filipino dialect, "*Putang Ina Ninyo Hayop Kayong mga Hapon.*"

The soldier grabbed the baby's neck and threw the baby on the ground. The soldier said, "The next time I hear your baby crying, I will stop it for you." Then he kicked her in the head until she was bleeding profusely. My grandmother moved next to her, comforting her. The baby's cries continued. My grandmother held the baby and tried everything she could to calm the infant, but there was no way to stop the baby from crying. She even tried to feed the infant from her breast, but there was no milk coming to feed on. Then one soldier rapidly walked inside, furiously growling like a dog, and slapped my grandmother, knocking her off balance. He aimed his rifle to her head, ready to pull the trigger. My grandfather crawled, reaching the soldier's boots, to have mercy and not shoot his wife. The soldier picked up the baby by the neck like a lifeless doll, and the mother quickly snatched her baby back, holding it tightly in her arms, but then the soldier swung his rifle, striking her in the head and making her unconscious. Again the Japanese soldier grabbed the baby of the unconscious mother. My grandmother attempted to go after the infant, but my grandfather grabbed her and wrapped his arms around her to comfort her.

On the wall was a crack wide enough to see outside. My grandfather was next to that wall, and he could see everything that happened. At that moment, he witnessed the most horrific, inhumane execution—an execution he'd never forget for the rest of his life.

The atrocious, angry soldier tossed the baby up in the air and struck it, piercing through its body with his bayonet. Shocked, my grandfather couldn't believe what he'd just seen. He thought it was only a cloud in his eye, but it was real. My grandfather closed his eyes, weeping and shaking his head. He could not understand why the soldier did it. He was very glad that my grandmother did not see it, otherwise she'd have gone crazy. The mother of the baby was still passed out when the soldier doused her with a bucket of water. Slowly she awakened and got up, asking for her child. Everyone in the room was silent.

She said, "*Para niyo ng awa Ilabas niyo ang aking Anak,*" meaning, "Please have mercy on me, give me back my child." The soldier laughed out loud, taunting her as he walked outside. She ran outside only to find her lifeless baby on the ground. She carried her lifeless baby, yelling, "Why?" She said, "*Bakit, bakit, Ano ang ginawa ng anak ko sa inyo,*" Meaning, "Why oh why, what did my baby do to you?" She added, "*Putang Ina Ninyo Mga Hapon, Hayop Kayo, Animal Kayo, Wala' Kayong Kaluluwa,*". Meaning, "You animal, you do not have a soul. Your mother is a whore, you Japanese." She walked down the empty street with her dead baby in her arm, drenched as rain poured down, yelling, "Help me, help me please, bring my baby back! Why, why, why, you animal *whore* JAPANESE?" Her voice echoed through the street. She walked towards the plaza, shouting, cursing, and asking for help. People could hear her cry, but they were afraid to come out.

My grandfather noticed the Japanese soldiers acting up in wrath. One Japanese soldier grabbed his rifle and went outside. Moments later several gunshots were fired, and suddenly everything became quiet. Everyone in the room looked at one another in tears, frightened by the loud gunshot.

One morning a Japanese official arrived unannounced and ordered the Japanese provincial officer to release the prisoners immediately. The Japanese were told to tail all prisoners to their homes and it would lead them to the Americans.

My grandparents were suffering in pain and traumatized by the extreme punishment by the Japanese soldiers but that would not stop them from pursuing what they had started. That night my grandparents crawled their way to the cave to inform the Americans of what was happening outside. The Americans were still recuperating from their injuries, but they were ready to evacuate with the help of the Philippine guerillas. The Americans were completely unaware of what was happening outside, and my grandparents spilled the bad news of what happened to Kapatan Danilo. The Americans were grieving and saddened by the whole incident, but my grandparents said it was not their fault. They said it was the right thing to do, to help and rescue the Americans. They swore they would do whatever it took to turn them over to the Philippine guerillas.

A week went by after their release, and my grandparents traveled to town to attend the mass on Sunday. Already the *Makapilis* were tailing them inconspicuously. The Japanese were everywhere and barricaded all the exits.

Inside the church, a little boy and his parents sat next to my grandparents. As the mass was in progress, the little boy extended his arm, passing the prayer pamphlets to my grandmother. There was a message from the Philippine Guerillas in it, "WE ARE COMING IN FIVE DAYS, RENDEZVOUS BALETE PASSAGE." My grandmother immediately placed the tiny paper in her mouth and swallowed it to avoid moles seeing it, but it was too late. Japanese troops walked in the church, pulling the boy and his family outside and likewise my grandparents. The Japanese questioned the boy and his family, asking what was the message passed to my grandmother. The little boy and his family denied wrongdoing and refused to give information to the Japanese. They questioned my grandparents about the message. My grandparents told the Japanese there was no message given to them.

Three shots were fired, and the little boy and his parents were killed instantly. The mass at the church halted as Father Edmund rushed outside to see what was happening. Father Edmund administered to the victims, but the Japanese walloped Father Edmund in the head, causing an open wound. My grandmother was shaken by the sudden death of the innocent family. My grandfather was speechless, comforting his wife. The Japanese announced, "Let this be your lesson that anyone aiding the Americans will suffer the same consequences." The Japanese let my grandparents go. My grandparents went back to the church to have confession as Father Edmund presided. Father Edmund was from Australia and had been serving the San Carlos parish church for many years.

Japanese maintained their presence, patrolling my grandparent's house. My grandmother told her husband she would leave at dawn to inform the Americans to prepare for evacuation in three days. The Philippine guerillas were coming and they would rendezvous in Balete passage.

My grandparents were ready for whatever consequences arose. They had already informed their children to be prepared in case they were taken dead or alive.

It was three o'clock in the morning when my grandmother escorted the Americans out of the cave to rendezvous with the waiting Philippine guerillas in Balete Passage. The wounded Americans handed my grandmother the map and entrusted her to take it to safety. My grandmother was surprised and asked them why they had chosen her to have the map and why wouldn't they carry it along with them since they were on their way to Capaz and the Philippine guerillas were by their side. The wounded Americans responded they were not sure if they would reach the safe location in Capaz, Tarlak, because it was a long journey and a dicey road ahead.

The Japanese were tricky and skillful at locating their enemy, the wounded Americans said, and they did not want to take that chance. My grandmother was skeptical, but she promised the wounded Americans the map was safe and would reach the proper authority to eliminate the Japanese from the Philippines. As they separated in Balete Passage, the wounded Americans were grateful for everything my grandparents and their children had done and for their uncommon valor.

It was already 1 A.M. when my grandmother arrived home safely. She bypassed the tight security presence of Japanese in the area. Her husband was scared she would not make it home, but finally she was by his side and they comforted each other.

My grandmother couldn't wait any longer and immediately she laid down the story to her husband. She told him she had the map. The Americans entrusted her with the map for safety, and it had to be brought to the proper authority. My grandmother begged her husband to take the map to Capaz and hand it to Philippine guerilla forces to be given to the Americans.

My grandfather would do anything for his wife, and this time he would embark on the journey to Capaz. He knew someone who could come with him and get him there as soon as possible.

One morning my grandfather left at dawn to Calasiao, Pangasinan, to meet his friend to come with him to Capaz. His friend knew someone hauling livestock once a week to Manila, and they would catch the truck and get off in Capaz. The road had many checkpoints, and they would have to blend in with the animals.

As my grandfather and his friend waited for the truck to embark on their trip to Capaz, breaking news rapidly spread and my grandmother was arrested by Japanese authorities and charged with treason. A *Makapili* man wearing a straw bag had identified my grandmother and her family as hiding the Americans.

The Japanese were on the lookout for the arrest. The Japanese had already sent massive troops to locate the children and her husband to be punished by decapitating their heads. My grandmother was shackled and brought to town. The Japanese demanded to know her family's whereabouts.

My grandfather went hysterical, begging his friend to help him to get his children in the Barrio. Luckily his friends knew people in the area and helped him to get his children out to safety. The Japanese dragged my grandmother to town and brought her to the garrison. Officer Tanaka ordered his men to unshackle her and escort her to his room. On the table was a stack of money to buy her out to tell them the Americans' whereabouts. Officer Tanaka stated that everything was forgiven if she would confess.

Officer Tanaka threatened her that if she would not cooperate with the Japanese, they would kill her entire family, including her friends and relatives. My grandmother did not back down and recited her rights, which made the Japanese officer furious, and he knocked her to the ground. She was defiant and resilient, and the Japanese had little patience for her unruly behavior.

The Japanese backed down, and the next day Officer Tanaka appointed a Filipino woman to negotiate and get her to tell her of the Americans' whereabouts; saying she and her family would be forgiven and rewarded freedom to do whatever they wanted.

Officer Tanaka, impatient, had enough and ordered his guards to put her back in jail. The town mayor asked my grandmother to give up the Americans' whereabouts because one way or another the Japanese Imperial Army would find them, and they would suffer severe consequences. My grandmother stared the town mayor in the eye and responded, "You are a disgrace and a chicken." The Japanese tried every which way of punishment towards my grandmother to unseal her lips, but she was tough and ready whatever the consequences. The Japanese ran out of patience and immediately dragged her to the town plaza and tied her to the pole. The whole day she was soaked in the sun, and the next day was the same. Her skin blistered and began peeling off.

The Japanese posted signs everywhere, offering American currency to anyone who could lead them to the Americans' location. There were rumored locations of the Americans' hideout nearby my grandparent's house.

The Japanese Army intensified their search and combed my grandparents' property day after day, tearing the house into pieces looking for information that could lead them to the Americans' where-about. Loudspeakers were placed in various locations to entice the Americans to surrender. The Japanese issued an order to shoot to kill my grandmother's family.

Officer Tanaka was being pressured by the high command and given an ultimatum to catch the Americans or he would be relieved of his command. Officer Tanaka ordered his army to detain anyone associated with my grandparents for interrogation.

It was Sunday morning when the Japanese soldiers paraded my grandmother inside the church and on the street with her hands tied behind the truck dragging her. As the vehicle rolled on the street, Japanese loudspeakers broadcast that anyone who could give information of my grandmother's family's whereabouts would be rewarded with five sacks of rice. Scorching heat left my grandmother's feet bleeding, marking the street with her blood as she was dragged to the plaza.

Interrogations continued at the town plaza auditorium for three days, and Father Edmund begged the Japanese to have mercy on my grandmother. One bystander shouted, "Do not tell them anything," and he was impaled to death.

The Japanese were running out of patience. They brought her inside the garrison and placed electrical wiring on her frail body and jolted her with electric current for hours, but it didn't work either. A rookie Japanese guard couldn't stomach the severe punishment of what his comrades were doing to her, and without hesitation, he stood up for her defense, brandished his rifle to his fellow Japanese soldier, and asked his comrade to stop the inhumane punishment or he would kill anyone who got near her. He reached the bucket of water and pushed it next to her. He untied her hands and helped her to sip water in her mouth. His fellow soldiers cajoled him to put down his weapon and he would not be punished. Otherwise his action was heresy and the result of this action was death by hanging. The other comrades, taunted him and called him "Filipino lover." The pressure built up inside the young rookie soldier as he aimed his rifle to his head and shot himself. The Japanese soldiers dragged the young rookie's cadaver and hung it on a pole, and attaching a sign that read "Filipino Lover" as the soldiers celebrated and chanted, "Bansai."

The harsh punishment continued in an attempt to persuade my grandmother to spill the beans on the Americans' whereabouts. They tied her feet up and placed her on a pulley upside down and submerged her head in a bucket of chomp, murky water, pulling her up and down. Again, it didn't work. One impatient, waspish Japanese soldier aimed his sub-machine gun at her face and murmured furiously with words in his native language. She just looked up at the soldier. The next punishment she received would be the Japanese pulling her nails off one by one.

My grandfather had gotten to his children in time and safely launched their journey to Capas before the Japanese soldiers could catch them. The children asked their father where their mother was and why their mother was not with him. He lectured his children and explained what happened.

The weather was not cooperating. They packed whatever they could carry and embarked right away. The children asked their father why they had to go to Capaz, Tarlak. Couldn't they just hide in the forest until the war was over? He showed and explain to his children what they were carrying and that it was very important material to be passed to the proper authorities so the war could be over.

The children were resilient, and it was already dark when they reached Balete Passage. There they found a safe place to rest for the night.

Their journey continued, crossing dicey roads and booby traps.

It was noontime when a grass shack appeared in the distance. My grandfather alerted his children to disguise and camouflage their bodies with mud. Marcial, the eldest son, crawled to check the location. Everyone was alert to Japanese activities in the area. Marcial signaled that it was okay. The children were excited to rummage the shack for what they could get their hands on. Everyone was hungry, but my grandfather was suspicious that it might be a trap. My grandfather stopped his children from entering the shack, but instead they stayed at a distance, awaiting someone to appear in the area because it was probably a trap. The children had already shared their last rolls of cassavas. A few minutes later, an old Filipino couple walked inside the shack with sacks of cassavas. The children rendered help to the old couple to carry the heavy load of their harvest inside the shack.

The couple kindly welcomed my grandfather and his children and offered them a hot meal. The children enjoyed the couple's grace. The old couple offered to let them stay for the night, but my grandfather was concerned the Japanese were probably nearby and didn't want the old couple to get involved. My grandfather explained they had very little time and had to continue to move on until they reached Capaz, the Philippine guerilla post. The old couple handed my grandfather a compass to direct them on the right path to Capas. They rested for awhile and resumed their endeavor in the afternoon.

After two days of treacherous journey, the youngest son, named "Ernesto," caught an illness. He continued coughing, had a high fever, and almost passed out, and they had to stop and rest before everyone suffered the same illness. The tempestuous weather contributed to everyone's exhaustion and sickness. They had to find higher ground to erect shelter.

Ernesto's high fever made him delirious. My grandfather roamed the forest to gather herbs to cure his son's illness. The children combed the area to find wood, tree limbs, and bamboo to erect a shelter. The sisters, Amanda and Angelina, took care of their younger brother Ernesto, monitoring his temperature by wrapping him with palm leaves and wet cloths to his forehead.

Everyone contributed to erecting the shelter, and it was shaped like a yurt. The other sibling, Tony, posted himself at the top of the tree, watching the surroundings for any suspicious activity in the area.

The shelter was plastered with palm leaves and they used skewered banana trunk as a flooring mat in case of flooding. Other children climbed the palm trees and grated coconut meat to make grease to use for frying, lamplight, and mixing medicinal herbal concoctions. The jungle was abundant with medicinal plants and creepy crawlers for easy snacks for the children. Right away my grandfather gave Ernesto a concoction of herbal medicine to take to lower his high fever and relieve his constant coughing. Ernesto rested quietly as the others improvised sharpened bamboo edges and soaked them in grease. As the sunset surged on the horizon, my grandfather said a little prayer to his family.

As the nightfall descended, Marcial volunteered to take the first watch as everyone was exhausted. It was a quiet night, and the clouds appeared to be retreating as the full moon emerged at the horizon. As the night grew deeper, Marcial's eye lids drooped. He roamed around to keep himself awake. He circled the shelter several times when suddenly a flopping sound emerged nearby. He investigated, but nothing unusual was happening. Again, the weird sound came from the dark. Marcial alerted his father to the strange sound. Together they scoured the surroundings, but nothing was unusual. His father said, "You were only dreaming. Let me sleep for a few minutes longer, and I will relieve you later."

Marcial left his father alone to rest, and he would wake him up later. He grabbed sharpened bamboo and hurdled his way up the coconut tree.

At the top of the tree, the view was breathtaking. He sat there staring at the horizon, imagining how it would be nice living without war, how it would be nice to be going to school, chatting with classmates, and having a friend or girlfriend.

He stayed there dreaming, lying down and comfortably stargazing, watching moonshine as the clouds passed through, covering the moon until it emerged again.

Out of nowhere, several large creatures appeared, reflected by moon glow. Marcial stood there wondering what he was seeing. He thought, *it's a large birds migrating, but it is impossible because the creature is traveling in the middle of the night.* He ignored what he saw and grabbed himself a young coconut to refresh his thirst. He tilted his head to pour the coconut juice into his mouth when the creature veered his direction and almost caught his arm. Marcial was stunned. *What the hell was that?* He tried to make his way down, but the creatures simultaneously attacked him.

Marcial fought back fearlessly with his sharpened, elongated bamboo spears, but several ugly creatures with fangs like wolves and claws like an eagle were no match for him. He tried to call for help, but everyone was sound asleep. He continued fighting by swooshing his long pole against the aggressive creatures, but he was overpowered and his elongated pole taken away. Quickly he grabbed his knife and cut bundles of coconut. Multiple drops of coconuts shook the landscape and awakened everyone. Quickly everyone grabbed whatever they could to fight the hungry creatures. Amanda and Angelina surrounded their ill brother to protect him against the unknown creature. Already the creatures were ravaging the roof to get their way inside the shelter, but Amanda and Angelina were ready to tackle whatever danger came their way.

Marcial yelled, "Aswang, Aswang, it's Aswang," as he slid his way down, scraping his chest as blood emerged from his body. The creatures sensed the blood dripping from his body and they intensified their premeditated attack to sip the red fluid.

Marcial saw the Aswang ravaging the roof of the shelter and alerted his father. My grandfather made his way inside the shelter and escorted his children out to safety. He picked several rocks off the ground and fired them at the creature. The creature had not backed down when Angelina lit the bamboo tip and tossed it to her father. He fired the bamboo spear into the creature, and the Aswang dropped like a bird to the ground. You could hear the baffling cries of the creatures as the others dissipated into the night and were never seen again. The creatures disappeared like a dust in the wind.

My grandfather said he had never seen anything like it before and he thoughts the Aswang was just a myth, but seeing it up close and personal was horrifying. He said there were rumors that many Japanese soldiers were missing or sometimes their remains were found mutilated by unknown creatures, but the Japanese always accused the Filipinos of cannibalism and retaliated by killing innocent people.

The family had a sleepless night watching the sky in case the creatures came back. Finally the morning came and everyone gathered their things and moved on. Ernesto was still ill, but okay to travel with the help of his brothers and sisters.

Day after day they persisted, and finally they were met by Philippine guerillas patrolling the area, who escorted them to the camp in Capaz to meet with Scout Master Gubatan.

Their persistency paid off. After grueling days of intense survival, my grandfather arrived safely and got down on his knees, his eyes streaming tears as he kissed the ground. Scout Master Gubatan kneeled, reaching my grandfather's arm and helping him get up. He shook his hand. "Well done, Emeterio, well done. I salute you," Scout Master Gubatan said.

My grandfather expressed his gratitude to everyone at the camp for the warm welcome and hospitality. Right away my grandfather asked Scout Master Gubatan if the wounded Americans were safe and rescued.

Scout Master Gubatan shook his head. He said he hadn't heard any news from his fellow guerilla he had dispatched to Balete Passage a week ago. Scout Master Gubatan asked my grandfather for his assistance in escorting his men to Balete Passage to rescue the wounded Americans and his fellow comrade.

My grandfather responded he would be honored to help the Philippine guerillas to Balete Passage.

Scout Master Gubatan had already selected a few of his men to leave at dawn with my grandfather to show them the location of Balete Passage. My grandfather confirmed with Scout Master Gubatan that once they'd reached Balete Passage, he had to go his separate way to take care of his wife's situation.

They were discussing the matter when eleven American commandos arrived in the camp escorted by the Philippine guerilla.

The commandos said they parachuted to nearby Mabalacat three days ago, and they were like birds of prey being shoot at in the air by enemy positions on the ground but they had managed to engage fierce fighting upon their landing. It was a hostile territory, and they lost four of their comrades. They fought heavily, dismantling the Japanese command post in Mabalacat and killing every one of the enemy.

The commandos freed several Aetas tribes that were imprisoned by Japanese soldiers. The Aetas tribes were so grateful upon being rescued by the Americans that the Aetas tribe vowed to help the Americans to fight the Japanese to the end. The Aetas tribe knew the area very well and guided the Americans in locating the Philippine guerilla headquarters in Capaz.

It was a relief for everyone in the camp that finally they had Americans on their side. Everyone applauded their arrival. The commandos hadn't had rest for two days, but they were happy to see Filipinos welcoming them with their hearts open. The officer leading the troops was Lt. Green. One by one, Lt. Green introduced his troops to a waiting crowd of Filipinos, who were in tears of joy to see an American presence in the area. Scout Master Gubatan welcomed the American commandos in the camp with warm hospitality.

Lt. Green mentioned a very important document the wounded Americans were carrying, and time was of the essence to recover the document. The American fleets were already in Tinian Island heading to Lingayen Gulf, just waiting for the command to engage and penetrate the enemy location.

Lt. Green said a USAF surveillance plane was returning to the base when a mishap occured. The tail of the plane was hit by lightning, killing one of the personnel crew instantly. They thought they had lost the crew completely, but a valiant Good Samaritan risked her life to help the remaining Americans by hiding them in a safe location. "That's what I was told," Lt. Green said.

When Lt. Green shared his views of the incidents, he noticed my grandfather crying uncontrollably. Lt. Green kindly asked my grandfather about his sobbing. Scout Master Gubatan instantly explained to the American commandos that my grandfather and his family were those responsible for risking their lives to help the wounded Americans. Lt. Green and company applauded the heroism and valor of my grandparents and their family in securing the wounded Americans to safety. My grandfather slowly unwrapped the banana leaves and presented the document to Lt. Green and Scout Master Gubatan.

Everyone was completely surprised and overwhelmed to see the map. They asked how he had acquired it. My grandfather told them it was his wife who received the map from the wounded soldier who entrusted it to her for safekeeping until it could be delivered to the head guerilla at Capaz or the Americans in the area. Lt. Green ordered his men right away to contact the base. One of the commandos had to stay behind to make sure the map would be picked up.

A messenger boy handed Scout Master Gubatan information, and he was dismayed by the news. His men he had dispatched to rescue the wounded Americans encountered Japanese soldiers and engaged in heavy fighting on the border of

Basista and Bayambang town. Out of the twenty-five men he dispatched to rescue the wounded Americans, ten were missing or presumed dead. The news was murky and they did not know if the rest of his men and the Americans were safe or taken prisoners.

Volunteer guerillas flocked Scout Gubatan's shacks, rallying to join to fight and rescue their comrades and the wounded Americans. He told the crowd that he had already chosen guerillas to travel back to Balete Passage along with the American Commandos and my grandfather to direct their way. They would leave at dawn.

Amanda and Angelina, his daughters, insisted they had to come along to be with their mother, but my grandfather refused to let them come because the journey would be dangerous and they would possibly encounter enemies down the road.

Amanda and Angelina expressed their rights, and if they would not bring them along, they would travel on their own. My grandfather was angry and insisted they stay behind.

Scout Master Gubatan responded, "Let them come along. They made it here safely, and they can make it back. They have a right to see their mother."

My grandfather said, "I'm worried, that's all." Amanda and Angelina clung to their father's arm and comforted him. The rest of the children remained in the camp.

Their journey was another drenching one. Constant thunder rattled the heavens. A man walked next to my grandfather and introduced himself. His name was Bu Wang, and he was from China.

Bu Wang and my grandfather chatted and became friends immediately. As their long journey continued, Bu Wang openly told stories of his wife and daughter. My grandfather just listened as Bu Wang elaborated the heartbreaking story of his family.

Bu Wang arrived in the Philippines from Canton, China, in 1935 to escape the Japanese occupation in his country. With his wife, Lucy, and daughter, Mimi, they settled in Tondo, Manila. Bu Wang was a martial arts expert. He taught martial arts to maintain his calisthenics, even though it was forbidden to extend the knowledge to others. Below his dwelling, he established a small noodle shop for his wife and daughter. Recently, Bu Wang's daughter celebrated her sixteenth birthday. He invited his neighborhood to attend the party with a dancing dragon to bring good luck.

Bu Wang was surprised to see new faces in the neighborhood crashing his daughter's party. He welcomed everyone in celebration of his daughter's birthday, but he kept his eyes on the uninvited guests.

Bu Wang's noodle shop was booming, and he continued sharing his knowledge of martial arts with others willing to learn free of charge.

For the past couple of months, Bu Wang had noticed the Japanese foreigners frequently hanging around in his noodle shop. Their arrogant behavior disturbed his customers dining in his restaurant. He confronted the Japanese foreigners and asked them to leave his establishment or he would call the authorities. The Japanese left without saying a word.

One day a frequent customer notified Bu Wang to hurry up to the school's front yard where the Japanese foreigners were stalking his daughter. He arrived right away and warned the Japanese to scram or else. The Japanese appeared insensitive and acted viciously. Immediately a brawl broke out and he knocked off his opponent without a scratch.

That evening, the Japanese arrived with an entourage. Bu Wang's wife, Lucy, begged him not to fight and to solve the problem diplomatically. He obeyed his wife's request, but the adversaries wanted revenge. The fight started when his Filipino student arrived to fight. It was a good brawl, and the adversary was defeated, suffering extensive injuries. Bu Wang's wife and daughter were worried the Japanese would come back with more of an entourage.

Bu Wang filed a complaint to the Japanese Consulate, but his affidavit had insufficient evidence. Bu Wang's life changed instantaneously as the threat against his life and his family continued. He cut hours at his restaurant and concentrated more on teaching martial arts to his pupils.

A month past, and Bu Wang took his wife and daughter on a trip to Baguio City to celebrate their eighteenth wedding anniversary.

One evening when they were resting, several masked men barged into his house and knocked Bu Wang unconscious. His wife and daughter were kidnapped by the masked men.

A regular customer found him unconscious. Immediately he was taken to the Chinese Hospital nearby. Flocks of people stood by Bu Wang's side, but his wife and daughter were nowhere to be found.

Day after day, Bu Wang spent his time looking for his wife and daughter. He begged the Japanese Consulate to return his wife and daughter, but the Japanese responded that they had nothing to do with his wife and daughter's disappearance. Every day Bu Wang combed the city of Manila, looking for his wife and daughter, but unfortunately found nothing.

The local authority was very little help to Bu Wang's case because they did not have enough information on the disappearance of his wife and daughter. Bu Wang became crazy and spent most of his time circling the Japanese Consulate. At night the Japanese Consulate gate was where Bu Wang dwelled, and the next day he continued his roaming of the Japanese Consulate perimeter. Other Japanese workers were irritated by Bu Wang's frequent loud calling of his wife and daughter's names, and others felt sorry for him. The Japanese guard tried to keep him away from the building, but Bu Wang persisted by gonging his tin cans to annoy them. Local police were notified many times by the Japanese guard to arrest Bu Wang for loitering, but they couldn't do anything because he was crazy.

One Japanese guard handed Bu Wang rice Masubi, and another Japanese guard saw the incident. The guard was relieved from his duty and never seen again. Bu Wang's health was deteriorating as he used a cartwheel to drag himself around to rummage trash bins. Every day Bu Wang stopped at the church in Quiapo Manila and stared at the altar, streaming tears.

One day Bu Wang noticed the Japanese staff were packing up their belongings. Trucks were parked at the back gate loading. The next day the Japanese compound was empty. The courtyard was solemn, abandoned. Usually the Japanese consulate was full of people and the guards were on duty. Bu Wang pushed the gate open and waited for someone to stop him from entering the premises. Still he kept his distance and looked around, and it was quiet. He dragged himself down inside the compound, hollering for anyone's presence. The place was completely empty as he helped himself inside to look for anything he could find to put in his stomach. At the trash bin, he was in luck to find unopened canned goods and bottles of Sake rice wine. He stuffed himself up and grew tipsy from the bottle of Sake when a plastic envelope caught his eye. There were Japanese currency and a letter inside the envelope. He immediately looked over the contents and pocketed the cash, then unfolded the letter to read. Bu Wang panted as he read the confidential memo. He discovered a letter from the Japanese Military Command of a massive attack on the Philippines and securing sovereignty under Japanese government.

Bu Wang took the letter to the nearest police station. All eyes stared at him because of his filthy looks and terrible smell. The police wouldn't let him into the police station.

Bu Wang handed the envelope to the police officer to read what was inside. He informed the police that the Japanese were going to make a massive attack on the country. The police officer didn't even want to touch the envelope. Bu Wang begged the police officer to see it or give it to his superior to take a look and read the contents. The police officer backed down to avoid the foul smell. All the staff at the police station ignored Bu Wang, kicking him off the premises.

In the far distance, an explosion erupted and everyone went to see what was going on. Bu Wang yelled out loud, telling everyone, "It's the Japanese attacking!"

The police were standing observing the explosion when a stray bomb took its toll, turning the police station into rubble. The attack was massive, and people were scrambling to find shelter. People paniced, stomping each other to get away, but the constant dropping of bombs from the buzzing zeros was too extreme to escape the blast.

Bu Wang heard a cry of children nearby. Without hesitation, he ran over to see what was happening. Hundreds of children were trapped at an elementary school. Teachers were trying to get help from the authorities, but they were caught by falling debris and killed instantly by bombs. Many children unfortunately vanished. The buzzing sound of flying zeros above was deafening, and the children all shook at the frequent loud bomb eruptions.

Bu Wang comforted the children and asked them to calm down. It was heart wrenching seeing children helpless and begging for their parents, Bu Wang said. The school building was engulfed in flames, and Bu Wang defied the thick smoke to find a solution to save the children. At the infirmary, Bu Wang scraped the Red Cross logo on the wall and used that piece to cover the children to evacuate them to the Japanese consulate. Even though the Japanese zeros were merciless killers, they respected groups of people, especially the children traveling and covered with a Red Cross logo.

The view of Manila from the Japanese consulate was catastrophic. Loud cries of people in the city echoed, and it was disturbing. Others tried to approach the consulate, but unfortunately the Japanese zeros already had their machine guns firing. Bu Wang didn't even notice—he was healed and saving the children. The oldest of the children was eleven years old and the youngest was seven years old. Bu Wang was surrounded by hundreds of children clinging to him. The consulate had enough leftover food to feed the children, but they had to evacuate the building at once because Japanese ground troops would be marching the streets. Bu Wang advised the children to obey his orders so they would get out of there alive. He appointed the older children to look after the young ones, and he said he would be back soon and had to find a boat in Pasig River to escape the Japanese.

It was 3 A.M. when Bu Wang awoke everyone and said to follow him to the river bank. The children were still sleeping, but he didn't want to take that chance because he knew Japanese ground troops would be flooding the streets of Manila the next day.

The smoke was still bellowing from the demolished buildings of the city, and Bu Wang took the opportunity to evacuate the children into *Bankas* or a boat, carrying them one by one.

Pasig River was littered with floating dead bodies, and the water was a murky stain of human blood.

Bu Wang managed to navigate the boat to Malolos, Bulacan, and finally they were rescued by Philippine guerillas who happened to be passing by in the area.

My grandfather praised Bu Wang's incredible courage and heroism saving the innocent children. Bu Wang was certain his wife and daughter were still alive and hoped they would be together again one day.

With such limited time, their dangerous journey afforded very little rest. When they stopped to take a rest, Bu Wang continued his impressive martial arts practice, and likewise my grandfather practiced his skills of *Escrima,* or stick fighting. They both taught each other techniques, and Bu Wang was totally impressed by my grandfather's ability to throw rocks and strike them in the air. Rocks were plentiful on the road, and my grandfather selected the right size of rock he carried all the time in his pocket. The American commandos scoured the areas ahead to warn others of booby traps and snipers. Bu Wang was unstoppable and moved like a monkey, climbing tree branches one tree after another, searching for the enemy's location.

On the fourth day of the treacherous journey, they reached the town of Bayambang, Pangasinan. Everyone had to be vigilant because of the enemy presence in the area.

Lt. Green signaled everyone to scatter. At 6 A.M. everyone was drenched and a heavy downpour blurred their visibility. Everyone stayed still, sensing any movement of the enemy presence in the area. Two guerillas appeared in the distance, signaling the area was clear. Everyone was tired and needed rest. Lt. Green told everyone to have a good rest but to be alert before it became too late.

People took turns on guard, and my grandfather and Bu Wang took the first watch. Amanda and Angelina were already snoring.

My grandfather roamed the empty building, picking up old pictures scattered and covered in dust. On a mantel a photo album was visible, though covered with dust. My grandfather held the photo album and viewed it page by page. The last page was a portrait of a couple, probably the owners of the house. My grandfather reminisced about the old days when he and his wife spent time with their children. The photo album reminded him how much he missed his wife, and he wished the war was over so he could be with his wife happily ever after. He placed the photo album back in its position and continued his watch. Bu Wang was on the other side, roaming the area.

As my grandfather continued roving the area, an unpleasant smell lingered like a rotting animal.

He checked the rooms on the first level, but nothing was unusual. He climbed to the second level, and the smell was unbearable to endure. Immediately he walked out of the building to have fresh air. He waved his hand to Bu Wang across the street to come over to his side. Bu Wang said, "What in the world is that smell?"

Bu Wang and my grandfather covered their noses with wet cloths to lessen the rotten smell entering their nostrils. They both went upstairs to investigate what was going on only to find a graveyard room full of decaying bodies. It was unbelievable to see the room littered with unborn infants next to their mothers who bled to death. Bu Wang and my grandfather hurried downstairs, speechless.

Bu Wang told Lt. Green to follow him; Lt. Green himself couldn't believe what was happening. At the end of the corridor, there was a growling noise and the door was ajar. Everyone cautiously approached the area when they discovered three juvenile females forcibly aborting their premature pregnancies.

Everyone was astounded. The place looked like a slaughter house with gore and bodies lined up, decaying. The three female juveniles were impregnated by their captors, the Japanese, and they escaped the compound while everyone inside the private house was having an opium session for their invited foreigner guest. The location of the private brothel was in the nearby town of Malasique. The private lodge or compound confined hundreds of young female captives abducted by Japanese soldiers as young as eleven years of age who were being forced to have sexual intercourse with special guests. The other abducted female juveniles inside the compound were Chinese and Koreans.

The two juvenile girls had aborted their babies, and they were only fourteen years old and bleeding profusely. Everything was rendered to help the two girls to stop the hemorrhaging but it was too late. The umbilical cord of the unborn child was still intact.

A girl name Elena survived the incident, but her unborn child was already gone upon delivery. She said hundreds of minor girls were abducted, held inside the compound, and raped. Many had been impregnated by their captors, and they were given herbal medication to induce or abort their pregnancies. The Japanese pictured the young wenches as sexual objects to satisfy their sexual needs, and after that, they treated them like animals.

Lt. Green and his men sat on the corner, speechless. They had never seen anything like it before; it was too gruesome and disturbing.

Amanda and Angelina were awakened by the commotion and quickly ran upstairs to see what was going on. Urgently Amanda and Angelina rushed downstairs, gagging. The scenery was too disturbing for Amanda and Angelina.

Quickly they escorted Elena out of the building. Lt. Green ordered his men and the guerillas to incinerate the building. Everyone was still recovering from the horrid scene.

Elena had been held captive by Japanese soldiers since she was fifteen years old. She said she was kidnapped by Japanese soldiers on her way to school, and her parents vanished without a trace. She was kept in the dungeon for six months by a high ranking officer, and every day she was raped by her captor. If you refused to cooperate with your captor, he would tie both of your hands so you were hanging on a wall, naked, and there he would do whatever he wanted to do to enhance his sexual pleasure. With Elena's pretty face and voluptuous personality, the Japanese did not waste any time taking advantage of her. As a matter of fact, the high ranking Japanese officer wanted to take Elena with him to his new post in Visayan Island when another higher ranking officer spotted Elena and ordered his men to take her away and be brought to his quarters. The Japanese officers dueled to own Elena, but both suffered extensive injuries, causing infection and death at the end.

After years in captivity, she was released blindfolded and transported to a place somewhere in Malasique, Pangasinan. The area was remote and located in the middle of the jungle, privately owned and operateded by rogue Japanese officers. The private lodge was for invited guest only.

The invited guests arrived blindfolded and signed secrecy papers. It was forbidden to reveal the existence of the location. The private lodge replicated the dwelling atmosphere in Japan. You could have young girls as much as you wanted, but you had to pay the price. The package came with the drug opium.

As time went by, Elena observed the sexual atrocity of the Japanese soldiers in the camp, and it was very disturbing. They called the place "The Devil's Camp" because all the Japanese guests were evil. The compound had two facilities. The first facility location was where they confined hundreds of young girls who were abducted. It had three Japanese soldiers and ten Makapilis. The second location facility is where the Japanese officers dwelled and spent their lavish life raping their victims—innocent young girls.

Hundreds of young girls were detained for sexual purposes only, and if they refused to cooperate with the soldier, they would be released out into the jungle and subjected to be a target for Japanese snipers positioned camouflaged above the tree tops. The Japanese soldiers were sadistic, using all kinds of things to satisfy their sexual needs, and sometimes it ended up in death by vaginal hemorrhages. The Japanese soldiers were sex maniacs and had no remorse whatsoever.

Sexually transmitted diseases were always present in the camp, and the Japanese soldiers used Sake to disinfect their penises after sexual intercourse. If the girls were pregnant or disease carriers, the Japanese soldiers automatically isolated them and immediately released them outside the compound, where they were terminated by the Japanese snipers. Every other week, fresh faces of young girls arrived at the camp, and all were blindfolded. Twenty to thirty minor girls arrived at the compound, and the Japanese officers flipped coins to decide who would be the first to rape their victim.

The Japanese officers had their way of playing games, having twelve naked young girls on the table and one naked man sexually engaging one girl after another, and if he prematurely ejaculated, he would be punished by running around the compound naked.

The Makapilis were forbidden to have contact or communication with the girls. They were there only to serve and follow orders from the Japanese.

Elena had been at the compound for three years. She planned to escape many times, but she hadn't the guts to do it because she had nowhere to go.

Elena begged the American commandos, the Philippine guerillas, and my grandfather and Bu Wang to help rescue hundreds of young, innocent girls being abducted for sexual slavery. She said almost every day young girls committed suicide but were replaced by more abducted young girls. The Japanese guarding the premises were drug addicts, and they were incapable of defending the place because they were all intoxicated from smoking opium.

Elena sobbed, begging everyone to do something because so many innocent young girls were being abducted and raped and used for sexual slavery.

Bu Wang approached Elena and asked her to describe the Chinese girls abducted inside. Elena said they were prohibited to talk inside the compound but a mother and daughter had been held in there for a long time.

Bu Wang got down on his knees sobbing, jabbing the ground as his knuckles bled. My grandfather comforted Bu Wang, calming him. Bu Wang continued his calisthenics of martial arts, releasing his anger until he was completely drained of his energy and cried like a baby. Then everybody agreed to go ahead and rescue the innocent girls at the compound.

Elena explained the location, and said it was surrounded by booby traps, but she knew a safe passage to get inside.

It was already daybreak when they embarked on their journey. After hours of treacherous terrain, Elena informed everyone they were close to the compound.

Amanda and Angelina maintained their distance behind their father.

Lt. Green ordered his men with the Philippine guerillas to attack the snipers at the tower. The job was well done, and they gave signals to everyone that it was clear.

They made their way inside the compound as the Japanese guard was busy flirting with the girls in the cage. Bu Wang entered the compound like wind—magnificently omnipresent and putting the enemies out of their misery.

Elena made her move, tiptoeing the corridor, as Bu Wang waited somewhere in the area like a ghost to execute his next moves. Bu Wang whispered to Elena not to be frightened, and he would be watching her all the way.

She continued her way to the cellblock when a Makapili appeared out of nowhere and grabbed her from behind. She was startled.

The Makapili said, "*Akala ko patay ka na, di ba buntis ka, bakit ka nandito,*". Which translates to, "I thought you were dead. You're pregnant, right? Why are you here?"

Elena acted normal and flirted with the Makapili man to draw his attention to her.

They continued communicating in the Filipino language, and she said, "*Bumalik ako dahil sa iyo*" (I came back because of you). The Makapili was excited and would have forced Elena to have sex with him, but Bu Wang appeared out of nowhere and slit the Makapili's throat. Bu Wang gave signal as everyone quietly made their way inside the compound and unlocked the cage where most of the young girls were captive. The healthy ones had their own, nicer cage compared to the older ones. Many were very weak from strenuous sexual abuse by the Japanese soldiers. Others had acquired sexual diseases and were isolated in a cell where they waited to die and have their bodies dumped in the moat.

The Japanese soldiers' atrocity was massive as young girls continued to suffer from various sexual diseases and severe punishment if they did not cooperate.

Finally Bu Wang reunited with his wife. With tears in his eyes, he held his wife like he never held her before. Streaming tears continued as his wife, Lucy, wiped his face with her hand. Bu Wang said, "This is like a dream; I can't believe it is you." He continued sobbing and asked about his daughter, Mimi.

Lucy told her husband their daughter Mimi was at the lodge with other newcomer girls.

Lucy told her husband the same Japanese men who hung around at their noodle shop in Tondo were now managing the private lodge and responsible for kidnapping her and Mimi and forcing them to be their concubines. They could not refuse the Japanese orders or otherwise they would be severely punished or even killed.

She said a truck loaded with Japanese officers arrived last night, and they'd chosen Mimi to entertain them. There were fifteen high-ranking Japanese officers staying at the lodge, Lucy said. Bu Wang cracked his fist. "It's payback time," he said. They escorted hundreds of young girls outside the compound for safety, but it wasn't over until all the girls on the other side of the building were rescued.

Amanda, Angelina, and Elena coordinated with the Americans and the guerillas to gather hundreds of girls and bring them out for safety. Lt. Green informed everyone to be quiet as they made their way out of the compound.

Bu Wang couldn't wait any longer, and he wanted to go ahead and rescue his daughter from the Japanese in the annex building. Lt. Green advised Bu Wang to wait until all the abducted girls were safely out of the compound, and then they'd go ahead and commence an assault.

Elena described the inn. The inn had fifteen rooms where Japanese housed their minor wenches, doping them and sexually molesting them.

Bu Wang quickly made his way inside, and was spotted by a Makapili guard, and he alerted everyone.

My grandfather continued throwing rocks, disabling the guard at the gate.

The American commando and the Philippine guerillas were valiant in eliminating enemies without gunfire.

The Japanese officer was still puffing the pipe of opium when Bu Wang and my grandfather entered the room. The guerillas and the commandos were in position to begin firing at the enemy presence. Other Japanese officers were caught off guard by the surprise attack and were clumsily running around naked, still stoned. Young, naked girls were delusional after being forced to use dope by the Japanese and did not know where they were. Bu Wang and my grandfather went room to room, searching for Mimi, but she was nowhere to be found when they encountered a Japanese Karate expert coming out of the room. Bu Wang dueled with the Japanese Karate expert continuously, and the young Japanese lad performed an unorthodox movement using various martial arts techniques. Bu Wang was impressed as he observed the man's movement to submit his adversary. My grandfather engaged using his Escrima, or stick fight, in helping Bu Wang, but he was no match for the young lad with martial arts style. My grandfather received several blows to his abdomen, and as he was on the floor struggling to ease the pain, Bu Wang said, "Let me take care of him." The fight lasted for a few minutes with Bu Wang's incredible techniques, and the young lad suffered a broken neck. Bu Wang appeared hopeless in finding his daughter when a voice was heard in the distance, and Bu Wang immediately recognized his daughter's call.

Bu Wang ran after his daughter's call, and the same Japanese man who bullied him at his noodle shop in Tondo was holding a bayonet knife to his daughter's throat. Bu Wang confronted the rouge Japanese soldier to fight him man to man. The rouge Japanese soldier refused to accept the challenge. He threatened Mimi, saying he would cut her throat if Bu Wang came any nearer. My grandfather was on the other side, waiting for the right moment.

Lt. Green tried negotiating with the disgruntled soldier, but he went hysterical, and Bu Wang tried to calm him down before his keen blade slit his daughter's throat. Diplomacy was Bu Wang's last resort for ending the confrontation. The Japanese soldier asked for water, and that was a big mistake. Bu Wang yelled to his daughter to duck, and my grandfather executed his amazing skills of throwing rocks off the Japanese's head, and it was a bullseye. The young rouge Japanese officer squandered, and Lt. Green finished the unfinished business by putting him down with his .45 caliber pistol. Lt. Green and his men were okay and likewise the rest of the crew.

Bu Wang was extremely emotional when he was reunited with his wife and especially his daughter, who was traumatized and suffering in a state of shock from the grim ordeal she's been through. Bu Wang wept tears of joy, introducing his wife and daughter to everyone. Amanda, Angelina, Elena, and everyone were emotionally touched and shed tears of joy for the reuniting of Bu Wang and his family.

Bu Wang chatted with my grandfather and said he was sorry that he couldn't come with him to San Carlos to help him rescue his wife. Bu Wang he had been so long searching for his family, and he thanked God that miracles exist and they were finally together again. He said that when the war was over, my grandfather could find him in Tondo Church every first mass on Sunday.

My grandfather responded to take care of his family because it was a one-time opportunity to be reunited with his family and that's an incredible story.

The separation was hard, but someone had to escort the hundreds of young girls back to safety. Other young girls were too ill to travel, so they had to improvise how to transport the fragile ones.

Lt. Green ordered half of his crew, along with the Philippine guerillas, to escort the young girls to safety. It would be a long journey to Capaz for the rescued young women, but they had to take their chances rather than stay in the hands of sex-psycho-maniac Japanese soldiers who sexually raped them every day.

They had to move right away before other Japanese troops arrived, and it would be difficult for everyone to evacuate. Lt. Green praised everyone as heroes.

Amanda decided to volunteer to help the young girls get back get to Capaz. My grandfather was sad because of his daughter's decision, but someone had to do something to render help to the weak, innocent victims. Amanda and Angelina hugged each others and each wiped their tears. The commandos and the guerillas set the compound ablaze.

Elena ran after Lt. Green and embraced him and my grandfather, her eyes streaming in tears, and she was speechless. The only words said were, "Thank you; you are my hero, my true warriors."

Lt. Green said, "I'll be seeing you."

They separated, waving goodbye as they ascended into the forest infested with unexpected dangers.

With Lt. Green and his men, they were six altogether, along with my grandfather and his daughter, Angelina, and seven Philippine guerillas on the way to Balete Passage.

As nightfall descended, they had to find a safe place to let the night slip away and continue their endeavor the next day. The sound of a roaring truck was heard in the distance. They carefully approached the sound of the vehicle, which was stalled in the middle of the road. The truck hood was raised as a soldier fixed the problem.

Lt. Green understood some Japanese language, and he could understand one soldier ordering his comrade to fix the truck problem immediately. Lt. Green ordered his men to take care of the matter and dispose of the bodies. The Philippine guerillas were in position, standing by in case of a worse situation.

They were surprised to see human cargo in a cage at the back of the truck. Six young girls, ages 14–16 years old had been abducted, blindfolded, gagged with cloth, and their hands tied behind their backs. They untied the young girls, who were hysterical, shaken, dehydrated, and hungry. The truck was on the way to the compound to deliver the human cargo, weapons, expensive booze, and plenty of goodies.

One of the commandos was an expert vehicular mechanic named Sgt. Mike, and in seconds, the truck was ready to roll. Angelina comforted the young girls, and she said everything was going to be all right.

Lt. Green asked Sgt. Mike if he could maneuver the truck. Sgt. Mike said it would be a piece of cake. Lt. Green ordered everyone aboard the truck so they could get out of there before enemies arrived. Sgt. Mike reversed the truck and hit the road.

Another truck came from the opposite way. Lt. Green advised everyone to be prepared to engage, if necessary. As the other truck passed by, the driver didn't notice any anomaly; it was already dark, and he just kept on going. Everyone felts relieved when a bridge appeared in the distance. Sgt. Mike asked Lt. Green what should be the next move: green to go, or red to stop.

Lt. Green told Sgt. Mike to take it easy and drive slowly. Lt. Green grabbed his binoculars and peeked through the viewfinder. There were eight Japanese soldiers guarding the bridge with machine guns. They had no other alternative, so they had to keep on going. He advised everyone to prepare to engage. The commandos and the Philippine guerillas ducked at the side of the truck, ready to commence firing. Angelina and the six young girls covered themselves flat on their stomachs.

Lt. Green ordered Sgt. Mike to turn the engine off and on, pretending the truck had engine trouble. Two Japanese soldiers approached the truck to assist with the problem, but they were instantly terminated, and the men quickly loaded their bodies into the truck, undressed them and took their uniforms to be worn by the Philippine guerillas to pretend to be Japanese soldiers. The Japanese guards at the bridge hollered to move the truck immediately or they would fire machine guns. Lt. Green ordered everyone to get ready to engage. Sgt. Mike gassed the pedal as the truck accelerated, creating skid marks, and they fully engaged with the enemy. Incoming bullets from the enemy zinged, damaging the truck's front bumper, but they were prepared and responded fast enough so the enemy met their fate. They successfully passed the bridge without a scratch. Lt. Green ordered his men and the Philippine guerillas to blow up the bridge and hurry.

They continued their journey, but the truck stopped in the middle of the road. The truck was out of gas. Nearby was a lake, and Lt. Green asked everyone to drown the truck.

My grandfather said they were close to Balete Passage. They'd find a safe place to rest for the night and continue their journey in daylight.

Finally they reached Balete Passage. My grandfather said, "This is it, we have to separate here. You take that road and it will take you directly to Balete Passage." The Philippine guerillas wanted to commence transmitting signals in the air, but Lt. Green averted the gonging right away because it would draw the attention of Japanese soldiers nearby.

Everyone had sad looks on their faces as they waved to say goodbye. Teardrops rolled down everyone's faces as my grandfather and Angelina parted for their way. Lt. Green praised my grandfather and his family for heroism, valor, and bravery.

It was already dark when my grandfather and Angelina reached San Carlos. The surroundings were completely guarded by soldiers, barbed wire, and satellite towers. Often the satellites circled the perimeter, focusing on any enemy presence. They crawled their way inside the church and waited at the confession booth for safety.

Father Edmund was startled when someone called his name. Father Edmund asked, "Who is there?" The call was coming from the confession booth. When he carefully approached the area, my grandfather slowly emerged from the dark.

Father Edmund almost had a heart attack, and he was surprised to see my grandfather and Angelina. They traveled through the secret passage and there they talked. Father Edmund explained to my grandfather that they were wanted dead or alive. Father Edmund offered my grandfather and Angelina a grace. They were very hungry.

Father Edmund asked how they had bypassed the Japanese guards. The area was surrounded with barbed wire and Japanese guard's shacks. My grandfather directly asked for Father Edmund's help to see his wife in the cellblock. Father Edmund said it would be suicide and impossible.

"Are you out of your mind? The Japanese are everywhere. I, myself," he said, "have been isolated inside the church because of this crazy war. I am only permitted to go to market once a week with Makapili escorting me to purchase my needs." The Makapili came every Saturday to escort Father Edmund to the market, and he was forbidden to communicate with the public. Father Edmund tried to soften the heart of the Makapili man to switch sides rather than betraying his country and his Filipino brothers and sisters by collaborating with the enemies. Lately, the Makapili man's heart was softening and he confessed to Father Edmund about why he sided with the enemy. He regretted everything wrong he'd done, but it was already too late. Father Edmund said, "Nothing is too late if you really want to change sides."

The people thought the person escorting Father Edmund on every Saturday was a servant at the church because he was open and didn't wear a straw bag to hide his identity. Only Father Edmund knew him as a Makapili, an enemy collaborator.

Father Edmund said the Filipino man become Makapili because the Japanese threatened to kill his family, and as a matter of fact, his wife was being held by a Japanese officer as a concubine in an unknown location.

Father Edmund assured my grandfather that they could use the Makapili to do good things for their side.

The following morning, they were having breakfast when someone opened the door and footsteps headed their way. Father Edmund tried to hide my grandfather and Angelina, but it was already too late. The Makapili man appeared standing in the hallway. They acted normally and offered him food. The Makapili man was suspicious and asked questions.

Right away my grandfather confronted the Makapili man and introduced himself. He told him who he was, and he begged him to help them. Angelina asked the Makapili man if he had a daughter. The Makapili man immediately broke into tears, sobbing. He said he had two daughters. One was fifteen years old and the other was sixteen years old, and they had been missing for the past three years now. He hadn't seen his daughter since then; that's why he joined the Makapili—to have privileges to look for his daughter and the Japanese promised him to find his daughter. His daughters were snatched on the way home from school in CeBu City, and he had never seen them again.

Angelina asked the Makapili man's name. He responded warmly that his name was Dodong. He was from Visayan Island off Cebu City. Angelina asked Dodong if he wouldn't mind describing his daughter. Dodong asked why. My grandfather explained to Dodong that they'd rescued hundreds of young girls abducted by the Japanese in Malasique. They were with the American commandos team and the Philippine guerillas when the rescue occured. The story of the rescued girls was heartbreaking. The Japanese abducted many young girls in different areas of the country, and they brought them to an undisclosed location to be raped and sexual slaves. Angelina assured Dodong that his daughters were among the hundreds of young girls rescued in Malasique, and they were safe now and on their way to a guerilla camp in Capaz. Dodong was emotionally disturbed by the news he received but he was so glad that his daughters were alive. He said the war destroyed everything he had in life, and there was nothing he could do about it. Dodong kneeled, walked to the altar sobbing, and asked for forgiveness from God. He asked Father Edmund if he would help them to get inside the Japanese camp to see their loved ones, would they forgive him and not reveal his secret to anyone. Father Edmund responded, "Everything is confidential and no one will know who helped." Dodongs periodically and apologetically sobbed and asked forgiveness.

Dodong had authority to come and go at the camp without being stopping by soldiers. He was a dedicated Makapili until now. He said tonight he could sneak them to the cellblock because the Japanese knew him very well.

Father Edmund said he had an idea: they would shave Angelina's hair, disguising her as a boy, and disguise my grandfather as a filthy beggar wearing a loin cloth.

That night they traveled inside the compound without hesitation. Dodong advised my grandfather to act as a stupid or crazy beggar on a leash dragged by Angelina, who was pretending to be a boy. Japanese soldiers liked the humor of a disgruntled human being. Lately the sirens had been going off and on as the American planes hovered above.

The guard escorted them to the cell. Dodong bribed the guard with American cigarettes.

My grandfather and Angelina were shocked and stood still for a moment before slowly approaching my grandmother. Dodong stayed guard outside in case other officers passed by.

My grandmother's health condition was fragile and she was blind. The Japanese had gouged her eyes out. Every part of her body was swollen, infected, and she couldn't move. It was just a matter of time before she would depart this world.

My grandfather and Angelina couldn't believe their eyes. They were filled with many emotions, mostly anger.

Dodong often checked on them and asked them to hurry up. "I'm sorry," he said.

My grandfather held his fragile wife's body, comforted her, and she whispered to his ears to put her down. She was very happy to have her husband and her daughter Angelina by her side. My grandfather said she whispered in his ear, asking if the Americans were safe. My grandfather responded yes, and he could see a little smile on her face.

Nearby a loud explosion erupted, and Dodong told my grandfather, "It's time to go." It would be difficult for them to see their way out of the compound. My grandfather and Angelina hugged my grandmother as she departed peacefully.

My grandfather wanted to take her body away, but Dodong refused to let him take the body out of the compound because it was too dangerous, and if the Japanese found out Dodong's dishonesty, his family would be killed. Explosions continued nearby, and Dodong and my grandfather made their way out of the compound. Angelina was nowhere to be found. She got separated from them. My grandfather wanted to go back to the Japanese compound to find his daughter, but it was too late now or everyone would be in danger.

Dodong volunteered to go back inside the compound at once to find Angelina before the Japanese found her. My grandfather was heartbroken, and he didn't know how to thank Dodong for his will and courage to risk his life for others. Dodong assured my grandfather that he would do whatever it took to save Angelina.

Dodong embarked at once and proceeded inside the compound. He acted normally and continued his search for Angelina. He went back in the area where they'd been, and Dodong could hear someone talking nearby. He traced where the voice was coming from, and he ended up in the Radio Communications Room, where Angelina was already being held and questioned by Japanese soldiers. Dodong and Angelina looked each other in the eye, and he made up a story that the little boy was coco. He tried to convince the Japanese soldiers that the little boy was his servant and he wanted him back to run his errands. The Japanese wouldn't buy his story, and instead they accused him of siding with the enemy.

Dodong tried everything he could to get Angelina out of the compound, but nothing worked—until an opportunity arose. Dodong and Angelina communicated eye to eye, and he moved closer to where the rifles were.

Dodong immediately grabbed the rifle, attached with a bayonet, and impaled the two soldiers to death. He untied Angelina, and they crept their way to the nearest exit. The area was completely guarded by soldiers, and the only possible way out of there was to get the Japanese soldiers' attentions. On the corner were two Japanese guards with machine guns, and Dodong overpowered them by slitting their throats with his Balisong Butterfly 29, a knife. Dodong was in position and loaded with ammo.

Then another soldier approached them, speaking in Japanese, when Dodong mercilessly stabbed his blade through the man's heart. Angelina was terrified by Dodong's behavior as he acted like a hungry animal, but he was determined to do whatever it took to save her.

Dodong asked Angelina to creep closer to the gate and he would take care of the rest. Angelina said to Dodong, "I am not going without you."

Dodong responded, "Angelina, you really look like my daughter."

Angelina replied, "I know she looks like me: that is what my sister Amanda said. And your daughter's names are Imelda and Carolina, am I right."

As soon as Dodong heard his daughter's names, he went numb and broke into tears. He was completely surprised to hear his daughter's names from someone he didn't know until now. Dodong hugged Angelina and he whispered in her ear, saying, *"Maraming Salamat sa pagtulong niyo sa mga batang inosenti."* It translates "Thank you very much for helping the innocent child." Dodong was still sobbing when he asked Angelina to go. A soldier at the tower fired a shot, and Angelina was hit on the thigh. Dodong cranked the machine gun lever and commenced firing at the guards in the tower, and they fell like birds straight to the ground. More soldiers were coming only to meet their fate. Dodong was unstoppable and continued firing and smashing the guard shacks, destroying their radio communication and the facilities. He was in control, killing hundreds of Japanese soldiers until he ran out of ammo. Angelina had already escaped the compound. Dodong's body was mutilated by Japanese soldiers dumped in the river. Traces of blood led the Japanese to the church. The Japanese ransacked everything at the church as Father Edmund was already tied onto the cross at the plaza. The Japanese continued their interrogation, asking Father Edmund who were the people who entered the church and why had the Makapili man turned against them. Father Edmund's mouth was completely shut, and the soldiers were going out of their minds. The Japanese commanding officer ordered his men to haul lumber and burn Father Edmund to death. Father Edmund sacrificed his life to save others.

The Japanese broadcasted their interests at the tower speaker, calling for my grandfather to come and pick up his wife's body. The Japanese stated that my grandfather and his family were forgiven and wouldn't be punished. My grandfather knew they were lying.

Again and again the Japanese continued broadcasting the death of my grandmother and insisting that some family had to come and pick up her remains. My grandfather and Angelina remained in hiding. A few days later, a constant blitz of USAF destroyed the Japanese facilities, and Japanese fatalities were mounting.

My grandfather received information on the location of my grandmother's grave. Her unmarked shallow grave was located at the riverbank. At 2 A.M. my grandfather smeared his body with dirt and crawled his way to the riverbank to find his wife's grave. The stars were bright as he slowly sneaked his way down the riverbank to be with his wife's grave. He lay on his back next to her grave, grieving with his eyes closed. Then suddenly a whistling noise was heard in the distance and struck the main Japanese garrison compound. The ammunition depot created a ball of fire, and he could hear the cry of the Japanese being eradicated.

American fleets had already commenced firing their big guns on Lingayen Beach until daybreak. People emerged out from their long hibernation and were already celebrating. My grandfather lay there talking to himself, and he could feel his wife's presence brushing his hair. Tears streamed out of his eyes, and he heard his wife whispering in to his ears, and the words uttered (he remembered) were, "We did it, my love: please take care of our children, and I'll be with you wherever you are for you are my life, my love, my everything."

All of a sudden he woke up and already American G.I.'s were everywhere assisting wounded Filipinos. My grandfather said it was like a dream. He closed his eyes, and when he awakened, the war was over. One American soldier name Cprl. Evans approached my grandfather and handed him a Hershey's chocolate bar and asked him his name. He said his name was Emeterio.

Cprl. Evans said he had heard that name before, but he couldn't remember where. Cprl. Evans asked who was in the grave. My grandfather replied it was his wife. Cprl. Evans was apologetic.

In two days, my grandfather was reunited with his family. Along with Scout Master Gubatan; Lt. Green and his fellow commandos; the wounded Americans Officer Waget, Officer Chelos, and Officer Anderson; Bu Wang and his wife Lucy and daughter Mimi; Elena and the hundreds of children they'd rescued in Malasique were among those present.

Lt. Green and Master Gubatan recommended recognition of my grandfather for his amazing valor, but my grandfather didn't really want anything except he asked for help to exhume his wife for a proper burial. My grandfather and his friends helped exhume the body of my grandmother, and to everyone's surprise, the body had repaired itself and it looked like she was just sleeping. All the swelling and bruising were gone and her eyes were completely intact. Her face was beautiful. My grandfather was astounded to see his wife totally different in death compared to when he visited her in the cellblock. Around her neck was wrapped a scarf, and when my grandfather unwrapped the scarf, they could see she was decapitated.

Hundreds and hundreds of people attended the funeral, and finally my grandmother rested in peace. My grandfather and his family never received compensa-

tion or anything from the U.S. government. What my grandmother wanted was to
save the wounded Americans.